Playing Together

An Introduction to Teaching Orff-Instrument Skills

by Jane Frazee

SMC 573

SCHOTT

Mainz • London • Madrid • New York • Paris • Prague • Tokyo • Toronto

to Steve Calantropio
Esteemed teacher, generous colleague, faithful friend

SMC 573

ISMN M–60001–049–3
UPC   841 88601 2448
ISBN   978-1-84761-149-9

Design, typesetting and music engraving by William Holab

Contents

---

* Pieces marked with * indicate the melody is sung.

All accompaniments written by Jane Frazee unless otherwise stated.

INSTRUMENTAL ABBREVIATIONS

SG . . . . Soprano Glockenspiel
AG . . . . Alto Glockenspiel

SX . . . . Soprano Xylophone
AX . . . . Alto Xylophone

SM . . . . .Soprano Metallophone
AM. . . . . Alto Metallophone

BX . . . . .Bass Xylophone
BM. . . . . Bass Metallophone

R . . . . .Recorder
SR . . . . .Soprano Recorder
AR . . . . Alto Recorder

Timp. . . . . Timpani

ACKNOWLEDGMENTS

After many years of teaching students of all ages, I concluded some time ago that codifying a sequential approach to building instrumental technique would offer much needed assistance to teachers who were faced with the opportunity—and the challenge—of introducing Orff instruments to their students. The many-voiced pieces in the *Music for Children* volumes were sometimes intimidating to Orff teachers, while generalist practitioners needed help in adding instruments to their curriculum offerings.

I had learned the importance of sequencing instrumental tasks from my young students, but when I was ready to write this book, I had long left the classroom. Fortunately, I found inspiring colleagues who were willing to comment on all aspects of the material presented and to give a classroom reality check to what I had developed. Their generous help has resulted in a work that has been vetted by master teachers who are in classrooms every day, a book that has been greatly enriched by their years of experience. In addition, all are experienced teachers of teachers, appearing regularly on Orff-Schulwerk teacher training programs and conferences throughout the US.

My admiration for the work of Michael Chandler, Cyndee Giebler, and Matt McCoy is matched by my deep appreciation for their gifts of wisdom and time that made this book possible. Michael teaches at Parkway Elementary School in Lewisville, Texas and he serves on the national board of the American Orff Schulwerk Association. He teaches in summer courses at Southern Methodist University in Dallas and the University of St. Thomas in St. Paul. Cyndee teaches at Blesch Intermediate School in Menominee, Michigan and writes delightful choral music for children. She teaches Level II in Orff-Schulwerk teacher training programs at Anderson (IN) and DePaul (IL) universities. Matt McCoy currently teaches at the Potomac School in McLean VA, and begins his doctoral studies in music education in fall '08. Matt teaches in summer Orff-Schulwerk teacher training programs at George Mason University and the University of Northern Colorado.

Further heartfelt thanks are due my sister, Kay Roberts, and my husband, Kent Kreuter, who kindly read the manuscript text. Finally, a gratitude encore goes to my *Orff Schulwerk Today* colleagues Wendy Lampa and Helen Peres da Costa for their support in bringing this new book to life.

INTRODUCTION

Following 50 years of Orff Schulwerk music education in North America, the curious reader may legitimately wonder about the appearance of a book that addresses a systematic approach to playing Orff instruments. Isn't that what teachers and their students have been doing all along? Hasn't the Orff-Schulwerk literature provided a wealth of examples of how to develop skill in playing pitched percussion instruments? Is there no progressive practice material available to lead students to technical proficiency?

The answers to these questions are mixed. The Orff-Schulwerk literature offers some help to the teacher who is eager to proceed in a way that best assures student success. We would look first to Gunild Keetman's *Erstes Spiel am Xylophon* and her three volumes *Spielbuch für Xylophon*, *Elementaria*, and to the five volumes of *Music for Children*. Yet, we must acknowledge that these books proceed at a pace that may not be suitable for the typical American classroom. Further, the examples are typically built on layered ostinati, and assume that students have the technical capacities to perform this rich texture at a basic level of instrumental playing.

After almost as many years of teaching and thinking about Orff Schulwerk as it has been present on the music education scene, I have concluded that a sequenced approach to the instruments might be helpful to teachers who are looking for step-by-step assistance in building instrumental technique, rather like an Orff version of the Czerny studies for piano students, but a lot more fun.

This book results from my conviction that what might be most helpful to contemporary music teachers would be to share what I learned from my years of working with young students: to begin with the magic of the sounds and to strip away the texture problems to concentrate on technical necessities. The result is a sequence that first approaches instrumental color through rhyme and song. Then we progress to mallet technique through playing accompaniments to teacher provided melodies. Two voices make music together, melody and accompaniment.

With the accompaniment techniques in hand, students can slowly proceed to playing melodies, and eventually melodies and accompaniments. Again, the texture is kept purposely thin to encourage concentration on technique.

Teachers who love the many-voiced orchestrations found in the *Music for Children* volumes may object that this skinny version of sound possibilities is not in keeping with the intent of our founders. I'm sure, however, that Orff and Keetman would agree that technical proficiency is essential for students to realize the wonderful music that they have composed, and—more importantly—to give students the expertise they need to improvise. Hence, the need for this book.

This volume represents a somewhat radical departure from the instrumental work that is present in the original Orff Schulwerk material. First, we encounter not pentatonic, but instead diatonic melodies from the outset. Such melodies establish the technique of hand alternation and crossing that also apply to pentatonic and modal material. The ostinato exercise patterns that are featured in all of the volumes of *Music for Children* are absent here. They can be introduced—and added to the instrumental texture—as the technical expertise of the students permits. Finally, songs with instrumental accompaniment are limited because we are working on instrumental technique; vocal technique is a separate and very important issue but it is not the subject of this book.

The book concludes with a section on playing instrumental pieces. For, as I cautioned in *Orff Schulwerk Today*, "instruments reduced to playing simple accompaniment parts lose their potential to explore melody, counterpoint, form and color. Students need and want to sing and play; I suggest that they ought to have the opportunity to do both—perhaps one independent from the other."

What you will find in this book are not exercises, but actual musical pieces; mini-etudes, if you will. They include folk melodies, authentic Renaissance music, a few of my own pieces, and selections from the standard Orff-Schulwerk literature. In this context, students have the opportunity to assimilate artistic melodic material and to use it to gain technical proficiency on the instruments.

Technical proficiency results from the way mallets are held, the way they strike the bar, and the flow of alternating hands when playing melodies. To promote a resonant sound, I encouraged my students to pull the sound out of the bars, or, with the very youngest students, to pretend the bars were hot. Remember that you are the model for expressive playing; the skill development of your students depends on your artistic example.

The inspiration for us all in this effort is Gunild Keetman. Her beautiful compositions and thoughtful reflections on performance practice have given us the spark of enthusiasm to carry on with our own students. This spark has ignited fires in the hearts of generations of teachers and students throughout the world. This book is my own very small effort to repay the huge debt we all owe to Gunild Keetman.

1. ENJOYING SOUNDS

Children's fascination with sound is evident even in the crib. Soon they are shaking rattles and bells and improvising rhythms on their mother's pots and pans. The toy store also offers an array of children's instruments of varying quality and electronic keyboards attract older emerging rock stars.

Orff instruments provide an irresistible acoustic alternative to these sound makers. Distinctive tone color, reliable intonation, and relative ease of manipulation invite teachers and even their very young students to explore unlimited expressive musical possibilities available on the barred instruments.

The first encounters use familiar rhymes and stories as sources for discovering the ways in which music can first enrich the texts and, ultimately, replace them. Ask the children first to speak the rhymes with you. When the sequence is clear, the stories may be told entirely in sound. The accompaniment to rhymes I've chosen can be played with only one mallet in the hand of the students' choice. All have been kindergarten Emmy award-winners in my music room.

Storytelling on Pitched Instruments

Jack and Jill
Jack and Jill went up the hill to fetch a pail of water,
Jack fell down and broke his crown, and Jill came tumbling after.

Tilt a bass xylophone against the seat of a chair with the high register on top. One student, Jack, stands on one side of the xylophone; Jill is on the other. Each holds a mallet in one hand. As the group says the rhyme, Jack and Jill proceed from the bottom of the instrument to the top. Jack falls down to a descending glissando. Striking the mallet on the wood is the sound of his crown breaking, and Jill glissandos after.

Humpty Dumpty
Humpty Dumpty sat on a wall, Humpty Dumpty had a great fall,
All the king's horses and all the king's men,
Couldn't put Humpty together again.

This story can also be told on a bass xylophone leaning against a chair. One child illustrates Humpty Dumpty sitting on a wall tapping his foot by playing one bar in the high register on a steady beat. Humpty's fall is a glissando to the bottom of the instrument. A few children repeat any note of their choice to portray the king's horses on xylophones (resulting in pitch clusters); others play the king's men on metallophones. Humpty strikes the lowest bar once on the bottom of the xylophone when he can't be put together again.

Little Miss Muffet
Little Miss Muffet sat on a tuffet eating her curds and whey,
Along came a spider who sat down beside her and frightened Miss Muffet away.

Miss Muffet sitting on her tuffet is portrayed in sound by xylophone players who select two repeated tones to represent "Muffet" and "tuffet." Metallophone glissandi play "curds" and "whey." The bass xylophone player will find three or four tones to repeat to represent the approaching spider, and the glockenspiels will scream (in ascending glissandi) as Miss Muffet is frightened away.

Jack Be Nimble

Jack be nimble, Jack be quick, Jack jump over the candlestick.

Jack returns without Jill for an encore in this simple story. The alto xylophones in their traditional position on the floor play the first phrase (*Jack be nimble*) by choosing one pitch to repeat as nimbly as possible. The soprano xylophones (*Jack be quick*) repeat a different note as quickly as possible, followed by the metallophone players who illustrate Jack jumping over the candlestick with an ascending glissando. Alas, Jack doesn't make it! The glockenspiels repeat a pitch of their choice to represent Jack's britches on fire.

Hickory Dickory Dock

Hickory dickory dock, The mouse ran up the clock,
The clock struck one, the mouse ran down, Hickory dickory dock.

You may choose to sing this rhyme before you introduce the instrumental version, but I suggest that you keep them separate in performance because the song and simultaneous realization on instruments are not likely to be a pleasing musical experience. Two alto xylophone pitches play a "tick, tock" introduction to this story, and during the "hickory dickory dock" phrase. The mouse running up the clock is a glissando on the glockenspiel. The clock striking one is played on a metallophone, a descending glissando on the glockenspiel represents the mouse running down, and we return to the alto xylophone "tick tock" for the final phrase.

Exploring Instrumental Color

The previous section on storytelling initiated the idea of realizing ideas in sound. We continue that idea by introducing sound substitutions for text words, with greater attention to the rhythmic content of the rhymes we consider.

The Giant

The giant is great
The giant is tall
But the elf on his back
Sees farthest of all.

This rhyme presents an opportunity to contrast the lowest sound registers of the bass xylophone and bass metallophone with the highest, soprano glockenspiel. The soprano metallophone may be added to thicken the sound of the elf. The bass players choose one sound to play the word "giant," the glockenspiel substitutes one pitch for the text word "elf."

Hey Diddle Diddle

Sound substitution for text words works well for this rhyme, but ignore the syllabication of the words, playing only one sound for each. Ask your students to suggest colors that they think might be best suited to illustrating the underlined words in the text. In this example, using different instrument colors and ranges such as bass, alto, and soprano xylophones and metallophones, and soprano and alto glockenspiels will help illustrate the seven different characters in the rhyme.

> *Hey diddle, diddle,*
> *The <u>cat</u> and the <u>fiddle</u>,*
> *The <u>cow</u> jumped over the <u>moon</u>;*
> *The <u>little dog</u> laughed*
> *To see such a sport,*
> *And the <u>dish</u> ran away with the <u>spoon</u>.*

Up the Ladder

This jump-rope rhyme combines the challenges of rhythmic precision with register awareness. Up and down must be portrayed by high and low instruments that illustrate the contrast, but the numbers and letters may be played by any instruments chosen by your students.

> *<u>Up</u> the ladder, <u>down</u> the ladder*
> *<u>A</u> B C,*
> *<u>Up</u> the ladder, <u>down</u> the ladder*
> *<u>1</u> 2 3.*

Old Pond

This example is sung, with spaces after the text to illustrate it with instruments. Metallophones might find two pitches to play "old pond," xylophones could play three for "frog jumps in" and "sound of the water" could be played freely as a sound effect on glockenspiels.

Basho   Jane Frazee

Spring Rain

Another song that welcomes instrumental comment after each phrase of sung text, *Spring Rain* will encourage your students to find ways to express rain sounds on their instruments. Unlike *Old Pond*, word rhythms are not a consideration here, but the length of the phrases that follow the sung text should be carefully observed.

Jane Frazee

2. PLAYING ACCOMPANIMENTS

From the beginning of their encounters with barred instruments, students ought to be encouraged to develop skills in a musical context. This means they'll be playing little pieces, not merely exercises. In order to accomplish this I encourage you to begin by working on instrumental accompaniments, since they are easier to play than melodies. When you play the melodies on your recorder or a glockenspiel, your students will be amazed at—and delighted with—the results of their first ensemble music experiences.

In order to play ensemble music, students must be able to keep a steady beat. I suggest that you prepare for initial mallet work by singing melodic phrases while they pat the beat with both hands on their thighs. When this is comfortable, they are ready to hold one mallet in each hand and tap the beat on the floor, as you sing or play improvised melodies or songs familiar to your students.

Finally the moment arrives when this skill can be transferred to pitch. Your students will strike two bars simultaneously, holding a mallet in each hand. Stems printed up in the scores indicate pitches played by the right hand, stems down are played by the left. I begin with octaves based on C in the following examples. You can simplify the task for your beginners by removing the bars adjacent to the high octave C.

I've chosen to present octaves first but, as Matt McCoy rightly points out, "the technique for playing octaves and drones is the same, so they could be used in alternation." Matt's observation makes the point that you will probably treat the presentation of the material that follows with some flexibility, selecting pieces in the order that best suits the skill needs of your students.

Hands Together: Octaves

German Folk Melody
Invite your students to listen to the content of the four phrases of this melody, calling special attention to the repeat of the first phrase at the end and the echo of the first two measures of the third phrase. The melodic structure suggests many possibilities for accompaniment, beginning with all bass and alto instruments playing together. Then they might change responsibilities for each phrase, as indicated in the score.

Ich spring an diesem Ring

This sprightly tune is attractive when accompanied by octaves on any bass or alto instrument, but it is especially enhanced if students can take turns playing alto xylophones and metallophones in the B section.

Lochamer Liederbuch (15th cent.)

All Around the Buttercup

This example introduces the special considerations of accompanying singing with Orff instruments. Invite the children to sing along with you and stress the importance of playing softly to support, but not overshadow, the voices. Remember to keep the accompaniment register an octave below the vocal range.

Trad., American

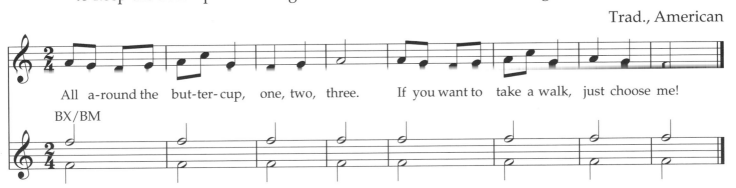

Green Bough

A canon written for older beginners, the texture of *Green Bough* is enhanced by the entry of the second voice in the second measure. The octaves are played on bass instruments to avoid covering the vocal line. Additional color may be added by playing glockenspiels on octave Ds on odd-numbered measures.

Chinese

Jane Frazee

Achieving satisfactory competence in playing octaves, we turn to drones. Drones in Orff-Schulwerk parlance generally refer to an accompaniment based on the interval of a perfect fifth. Because the following examples illustrate melodies with four different tonal centers, each drone is built on a different tonic pitch. You will need to remove bars adjacent to the drone pitches to help your students avoid playing unwanted sounds.

Hands Together: Drones

Filles à Marier

Here is a wonderful opportunity to distinguish the sounds of different color families. After you have played the melody on your recorder, try it on a soprano instrument (xylophone, metallophone, or glockenspiel), as your students play the drone on alto instruments of the same color. Or you can contrast registers by playing the piece on low instruments, then on glockenspiels, being careful to keep the melody and accompaniment an octave apart.

Library of Bourgogne (c. 1450)

Triory de Bretagne

If you play this lively tune on your soprano recorder, your students might like the sound of drones on alto xylophones and metallophones. Or they could contrast metal with wood accompaniments on each of the two phrases, or contrast bass with alto instruments taking turns in alternate measures.

Orchesographie (1588)

Latvian Lullaby

We encounter the special consideration of accompanying vocal melodies again in this piece. The drone will need to be played softly on bass instruments, supporting the children's voices an octave below the vocal range. Or you could make it an instrumental piece and transpose all parts up an octave.

Trad., Latvian

Lull - a - by my dear one, Soft-ly sleep my child,   Sis-ter gent-ly rocks you, Warm her hands and mild.

Moonrise

The flattened second scale degree at the cadence of this piece creates a melody in the Phrygian mode. If you want your students to sing this composition in Aeolian, simply substitute an F♯ for the F♮. Obviously intended for older students, the drone will be played on bass instruments and contains a bit of rhythmic interest, absent in our previous examples.

Anon.

Jane Frazee

Hands in Alternation: Octaves

Here we encounter our first technical leap—from simultaneous hand movement (conjunct motion) to hands separated (disjunct motion). Mastering this new challenge is a prerequisite for playing ostinato parts that are the foundation of elemental style and for learning to play melodies on the instruments.

Breton Folk Melody

I suggest that you practice this accompaniment by ignoring the half-beat rests in the score and simply repeat the first measure. When this is secure, ask your students to play the first three notes as written, then tap the right-hand mallet on their shoulders. Try experimenting with different instruments here, remembering to keep the melody an octave above whatever accompaniment instrument you select.

Trad., French

Keetman Piece #8 (from *Erstes Spiel am Xylophon*)

In her many works for xylophone, Keetman does not always indicate mallet alternation preferences (stems up for right hand, stems down for left), but this book is an exception. While I offer this piece as an accompaniment example, I urge you to revisit it later when you undertake melody-playing on the barred instruments, following Keetman's mallet indications. This is a generous piece—actually three little pieces in one—so pick the one you like the best and enjoy it with your students.

Gunild Keetman

Branle

This branle (or brawl in English) is accompanied by a four-measure ostinato. Practice it first without the third measure rhythm challenge, adding it when the meter is secure. Finger cymbals or a tambourine on the downbeat of each measure adds to the effect of this lively dance.

Orchesographie (1588)

When the Sun Wakes Up

An alarm (perhaps an insistent triangle) might introduce this piece. Practice the accompaniment at first by playing F octaves as illustrated in the second measure. When the tune is familiar add the rests on every other measure as indicated in the score. While a second voice is added in the score, you may choose to perform this piece in unison to concentrate on the accompaniment. Between repeats of the song, your students will love to tell you what they think the day's surprise might be.

Jane Frazee

When the sun wakes up___ it's time to rise,

When the sun wakes up___ it's time to

O - pen your eyes for the day's___ sur - prise. Sur - prise!

rise, O - pen your eyes for the day's___ sur - prise.

Hands in Alternation: Drones

Begin the disjunct motion practice with conjunct in the following examples. First, ask students to practice hand alternation on their thighs. Next, at the instruments, play the drone as if it were a chord, then separate the pitches as indicated in the score. This new motor movement is the initial step to playing arpeggiated drones, and it prepares for later playing of increasingly challenging rhythmic ostinato parts.

Ungaresca

A broken drone is an ideal accompaniment to this lively Mixolydian melody. You can begin by playing half notes in each measure, then try quarter notes (D-A-D-A) when your students are ready for a more difficult challenge. Alternatively, you can begin your melody at a slow tempo with half-note accompaniment, then accelerando with each melodic repetition.

Pierre Phalèse (c. 1550)

Long Summer Day

The **A A′** structure of this American folk song suggests that unpitched percussion colors might be added to punctuate the form. As notated, the broken drone enhances the melodic character and intensifies the forward motion of the piece.

Trad., American

Rock-y road to Geor-gia on a long sum-mer day, Rock-y road to Geor-gia on a long sum-mer day.

Tourdion Basse Dance

This triple meter piece poses a special problem for an early encounter with the broken drone because rhythmic considerations (half note followed by quarter note in each measure) demand the player's attention. Mastery of this challenge indicates that your students will soon be ready to attempt rhythmically demanding ostinato patterns.

Attaingnant Dance Prints (c. 1550)

Whistle Daughter Whistle

The melodic material of this folk song is a repeated four-measure phrase. The broken drone accompaniment is actually a two-measure ostinato. It might be enhanced by changing the second beat of alternate measures to two eighth notes, played by the right hand.

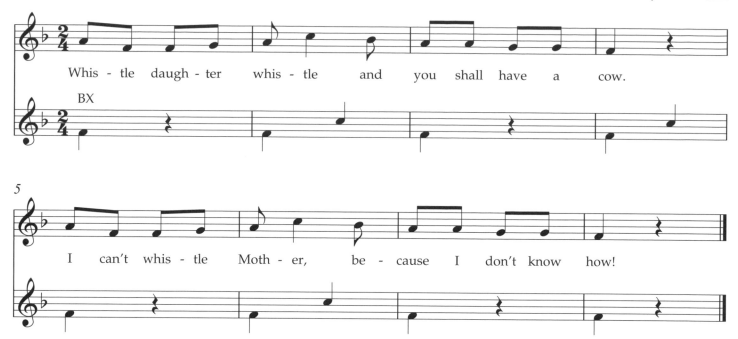

Hands Together: Moving to Adjacent Pitches (Octaves)

The introduction of pieces that require simultaneous hand movement from one bar to another is the beginning of instrumental facility. The examples that follow illustrate only two of the many possibilities for this kind of movement.

Instrumental Piece (from *Music for Children II*)

This serene piece should be played slowly and gently. Originally written to be accompanied by water glasses, the alto metallophone is an acceptable substitute. Adding the chord thirds fills out the texture and conveys the intended Orff/Keetman sound.

Orff/Keetman
arr. Jane Frazee

Elizabethan Inspiration

The octave movement here is accessible for relatively inexperienced players because it moves slowly. The soprano recorder melody can be accompanied by alto or bass instruments. The accompaniment is a four-measure repeated phrase.

Jane Frazee

Hands Together: Moving to Adjacent Pitches (Fifths)

Once again we move from the interval of the octave to the fifth. The first melody that follows is supported by hands moving up; the hands move down in the second. In addition, ostinato and rhythm become factors in these accompaniments.

Lullaby

If you choose to sing this melody on "loo" while your students accompany you on their instruments, the fifths will be played on bass instruments. However, if you play your soprano recorder, alto xylophones and metallophones would provide appropriate support. Perhaps you could try both options in performance, contrasting the instrumental with the vocal version.

Jane Frazee

Prendes I garde

You'll notice that the accompaniment for this old tune is an ostinato—the first two measures are repeated. This sounds to my ears like a recorder melody, but other realizations are possible. I might be tempted to enhance the texture with a hand drum playing a skipping rhythm (♩ ♪).

13th cent. Trouvère Melody

Moving Drone: Fifth Moves

The subtle introduction of harmonic movement in Orff Schulwerk literature begins with the embellishment of the fifth in ascending or descending fashion. In this case, only the right hand moves while the left remains static. Since practice on the thighs prepares for transfer to the instruments, begin with patting right and left simultaneously, then move the right hand onto the floor to the right and back to the thigh, then to the floor on the left of the thigh and back. Introduced in Volume II of *Music for Children*, this movement typically occurs on unaccented beats of the measure. It evokes a particularly poignant quality in instrumental and vocal pieces.

Instrumental Piece #1 (from *Music for Children II*)
The **a a b/b a** form of this gentle piece is accompanied by a one-measure ostinato. Written for glockenspiels, you might want to assign the accompaniment parts to other instruments and play the melody on your soprano/alto recorder or barred instrument of your choice, remembering to observe the octave distance between melody and accompaniment.

Orff/Keetman

Roses
The changing rhythm of this melody requires an accompaniment that acknowledges and supports it. The accompaniment is written as an ostinato so that the embellishment of the fifth occurs on the weak beat of the triple meter measures. Prepare this by thigh-patting, asking half the group to pat the ostinato accompaniment while the other half sings, then reverse the tasks.

I tend my rose bush ev-'ry day, I tend my rose bush ev-'ry day, It buds and

blos - soms ev - 'ry May, It buds and blos - soms ev - 'ry May.

No Sky at All

The fifth moves up in this example, which your students can prepare on their thighs before they attempt to play it on the bass metallophones. If you want alto instruments involved, you should perform the melody on your soprano recorder. You might ask the students to perform the ostinato on their thighs while singing the melody.

Shiki   Jane Frazee

No sky at all, No sky at all, No sky, still the snow - flakes_ fall, No sky at all.

Moving Drone: Tonic Moves

Rather fewer examples of the moving tonic than moving fifth are found in elemental style because it can weaken the sense of tonality if not confined to a weak beat. Your students will practice this movement by keeping the right hand on the right thigh, while the left moves from the floor to the left thigh.

Melody from Piece #11 (from *Music for Children II*)

Here is a simplified version of a piece written for glockenspiels in the Orff/Keetman literature. The absence of rhythmic considerations makes this an easy piece to begin the movement of the left hand from the tonic to the supertonic, while the right hand remains solidly anchored on the fifth.

Ring Around the Rosie

The accompaniment here becomes a two-measure ostinato because of the rhythmic tension of the movement away from the tonic on the third of the four-beat accompaniment pattern. Divide your group's responsibilities between singing the familiar tune and patting accompaniment, which will soon be transferred to bass xylophones.

Trad., American

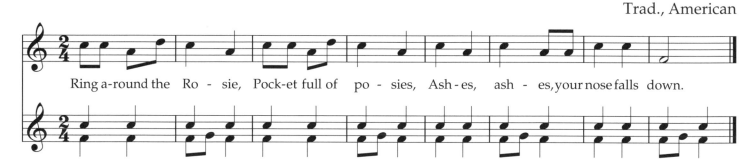

Ring a-round the Ro - sie, Pock-et full of po - sies, Ash - es, ash - es, your nose falls down.

Dominant Shift: Drone Moves to Dominant Octave

Because it is rare to find a melody in which the shift to the dominant occurs on alternate measures, this maneuver is found typically in the context of a phrase. The melodic form is highlighted by the shift as illustrated in the following examples. Preparation for this accompaniment begins by patting both hands on thighs, then move the left to the floor to simulate the move to the dominant.

Babylon's Falling

This little folk song is an ideal first experience for beginning players. The accompaniment involves only one phrase and there are no rhythmic challenges in either melody or accompaniment.

Trad., American

Bab-y-lon's fall-ing, fall-ing, fall-ing, Bab-y-lon's fall-ing to rise no more.

British Folk Song

In this example we confront three melodic phrases, the first and last are repeated, with a slight variation in measure 9. But the dominant shift in the second phrase is a two-measure repeated pattern, in contrast to the four-measure accompaniment of the first and last phrases. I suggest that you begin by preparing the first and last phrases, adding the second phrase when this is secure.

Trad., British

Didn't My Lord

The syncopation in this melody suggests that it will be appropriate for older beginners. Cyndee Giebler provided this stylistically appropriate accompaniment that enhances the melodic rhythm. Your students will need to practice the syncopated bass xylophone part on their thighs while you sing the melody. If they are sitting in a circle they can practice the dominant shift by moving their left hands to their neighbor's right thigh (always an interesting diversion for older students). Eventually the group will sing the tune accompanied by a student playing bass xylophone.

American Spiritual
arr. Cyndee Geibler

Did-n't my Lord de - liv-er Dan - iel,___ de-liv-er Dan - iel,___ de-liv-er Dan - iel?___ Did-n't

my Lord de - liv - er Dan - i - el so why not___ ev - e - ry - one?

Hand Crossing: Left Crosses, Right Stable

Hand-crossing accompaniments in elemental style are called arpeggiated drones and they prepare the way for playing melodies on barred instruments. They can be prepared by thigh-patting and instrumental gestures that simulate the hand-crossing patterns to follow.

Pat two hands on the left thigh, then pat just the right hand on the left thigh while the left crosses over to the right. Transfer to the instruments looks like this:

Instrumental Piece #29 (from *Music for Children I*)

This little piece for glockenspiels can be realized by any number of instrumental combinations, but I suggest that you begin with a bass or alto instrument with your inexperienced players because larger bars are easier to play than smaller ones. You can play the melody on your recorder or a glockenspiel while you simultaneously cross your fingers for the success of your students as they attempt their first hand-crossing accompaniment.

Folk Dance

A piece written by Isabel Carley intended for performance on alto recorder and bass xylophone with added unpitched percussion for rhythmic interest, this delightful piece is a textbook example of an arpeggiated drone accompaniment. It is the A section of a two-part form.

Isabel Carley

Down Came a Lady

The arpeggiated drone adds a bit of welcome rhythmic tension to the accompaniment for this little folk song, occurring as it does only every other measure. You might prepare it with the text:

Down, up Down up ov - er

Another text possibility, suggested by Cyndee Giebler, is "low, high, now jump over."

Trad., American

Down came a la - dy, Down came two,

Down came Lord Dan - iel's wife and she was dress'd in blue.

Hand Crossing: Right Crosses, Left Stable

The preparation for this challenge is just the reverse of what we've practiced above. Pat two hands on the right thigh, then pat just the left hand on the right thigh while the right crosses over to the left. Transfer to the instruments looks like this:

Cut the Cake

This is a very simple hand-crossing exercise without rhythmic complications. The folk melody and text suggests that this might be a first experience for your beginning players.

Trad., American

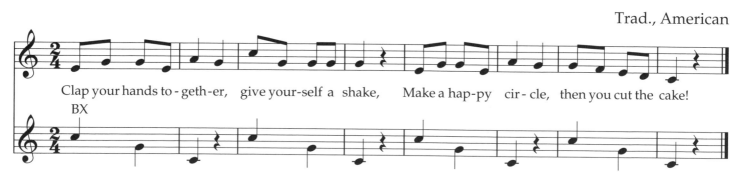

Clap your hands to - geth - er, give your-self a shake, Make a hap-py cir - cle, then you cut the cake!

Melody from Ostinato Piece #7 (from *Music for Children II*)

As you pat the accompaniment pattern, you might add a text like the one we used for *Down Came a Lady* above. In this case, say "up, down, up down over."

Orff/Keetman
accomp. Jane Frazee

3. PLAYING MELODIES

The variety of accompaniments that your students have encountered in the preceding pieces has provided the essential technical background for playing melodies on barred instruments. The particular difficulties that students will encounter in melody-playing are hand-crossing and spatial orientation; melodies typically occur in more limited spaces than do accompaniments. Consideration of instruments is also important; for example, the color of glockenspiels makes them well suited to playing melodies, but the small size of the bars can make this difficult for young players. Choosing melody instruments with care can help your students succeed in these new, challenging and rewarding opportunities for music-making.

The following examples are presented without accompaniment in order to identify and practice melodies that feature steps, skips, repeated notes, and combinations of each. However, you can enhance the sound by adding appropriate accompaniments already practiced if you want to enrich the musical experience of your players.

Stem direction is important here: downward stems are played by the left hand, the right hand plays those printed up. However, like fingering in piano music, different solutions are possible and you should experiment to find your own favorite sticking options. I've also chosen to flaunt the sometimes practiced Orff-Schulwerk convention of alternating mallets on successive pitches, following the example of Gunild Keetman. For, as Michael Chandler points out, there is evidence on the DVD devoted to Keetman's work that she often played G and A with the right hand, and C, D, and E with the left.

Finally, I've attempted to organize the pieces according to difficulty but, as I suggested earlier, you'll want to select those examples that best address the technical needs of your different age groups.

Steps

I have chosen C as the key center for these first encounters with melodies that move by step. *Come Be Merry* works as a canon if your students can play it with rhythmic accuracy. I suggest that you eliminate the first and last two measures of *La Cloche* as you practice the step-wise movement, adding them at the end. It is a wonderous accomplishment for your students to play this piece in canon! Finally, *Sleepy Head* will be easier to master if you omit the last two beats of the fourth measure until both phrases are secure.

One Step at a Time

Jane Frazee

Come Be Merry

Old Melody

La Cloche

Trad., French

Sleepy Head

Jane Frazee

Skips

We take a huge leap in technical expectations when we introduce skips! How large should the intervals be? Should the material be pentatonic, allowing bars to be removed? Should hands cross in the execution of the skip? I've included examples that address all of these questions in the material that follows.

The Absent F

This little piece introduces the skip of a third in a pentatonic context. Note that hands do not alternate on each pitch; the last beat of each measure and the first of the next are both played by the left hand.

Jane Frazee

Peter Peter Pumpkin Eater

A familiar tune for black-key piano players, this works just as well on bar instruments set up in pentatonic. You might want to begin with the right-hand movement only, then it will cross over the left which is stationed on C. It's also fun to change hands, beginning with the left, to get a different sensation of the crossing experience.

Trad., American

(Repeat 3x)

Crooked Man

An opportunity to practice both steps and skips is provided here. The right hand remains stationary throughout the first section as the left skips over, making the negotiation of the diatonic melody fairly comfortable. Practice the last phrase in quarter notes before attempting the melodic rhythm as printed.

Trad., American

The B Section

A hexatonic melody with no repetitions, this melody is built on skips of thirds. Practicing the first and third beats of each measure first will give your students a general sense of the direction of the melody that they will soon play.

Elizabethan Melody
adap. Jane Frazee

Repeated Notes

Playing repeated notes requires considerable dexterity, especially at quick tempos. I have indicated same or alternate mallet-playing depending on the musical context, but you may choose different alternatives for your students.

The A Section

Your students have already learned the B section of this piece! Here they play a melody that begins with repetition on every measure.

Elizabethan Melody
adap. Jane Frazee

Keetman Piece #12 (from *Discovering Keetman*)

Keetman here suggests alternating mallets on each pitch for rhythmic fluency. Following her indications for mallet-playing will encourage you to play this piece at a lively tempo.

Keetman's accompanying ostinato alternates high C in the right hand with C D E G on the beat in the left.

Gunild Keetman

Melody #17 (from *Music for Children I*)

With the exception of skips at the beginning of almost every measure, this example, with its mallet alternation, offers the opportunity to play repeated notes at a fairly brisk tempo. You might try a broken drone on the beat if you choose to accompany this piece, or see the more challenging ostinati on page 104 of *Music for Children I*.

Orff/Keetman

Ungaresca

Here is another contribution from the 16th-century composer Pierre Phalèse. The mallet indications in the second section provide an optional opportunity to practice the same motive with opposite mallets (the first measure begins with the left, the third with the right). As indicated in the section on accompaniments, these Phalèse dances are often performed with an accelerando on each repetition of the melody.

Pierre Phalèse

Steps, Skips, and Repeated Notes

Branle de Champaigne

While this melody at first glance seems extended, it is actually only two four-measure phrases repeated. I would practice the B section by playing first the odd-numbered measures followed by the more rhythmically active even-numbered measures. Try a contrast of wood and metal tone colors for each section when performing this piece.

Keetman Piece #8 (from *Spielbuch für Xylophon I*)

The tonal center of this interesting pentatonic piece is not *do*, but *mi*. Note that Keetman suggests mallet repetition at the outset of measures one and three and at the end of measures two and eight. Even more interesting, the echo of measure five in measure six is played by the left hand, while measure five is played by the right. If you are moved to accompany this piece, please do not play a drone based on E (E and B), but octave Es would be acceptable until the little coda.

Gunild Keetman

Keetman Piece #22 (from *Erstes Spiel am Xylophon*)

When Keetman writes pieces that alternate mallets on every pitch, I suggest that she probably has a fairly quick tempo in mind. If you choose to add a drone accompaniment, you could change from the drone on the beat to the division of the beat (eighth notes) on the repeat of the melody, following Keetman's example.

Gunild Keetman

Keetman Piece #27 (from *Spielbuch für Xylophon I*)

A pentatonic melody based on *la*, this extended piece is written in **A B C A** form. I suggest that you practice the right hand alone in the B and C sections to learn the shape of the melody, adding the after-beats when that is secure. Or, if you choose to present the piece in a more approachable manner, you might play it omitting the B or the C section. While the score indicates only right hand for measures 3 and 4, I encourage you to continue mallet alternation for fluency.

Gunild Keetman

4. PLAYING TWO-PART INSTRUMENTAL PIECES

The following examples offer your students the opportunity to combine melodies and accompaniments. They have now mastered the technical proficiency necessary to perform these pieces in their previous encounters with melody and accompaniment. You can select the ensemble instruments based on your conception of tempo, character of the music, and ages of your student performers. Enjoy!

Canon #37 (from *Music for Children I*)
This clever canon is essentially one phrase repeated four times and will be easily mastered if you teach it in unison, introducing the counterpoint when the melody is secure.

Orff/Keetman

Pavan
For stylistic reasons, the melody, played by two alto xylophones, should be enhanced by soprano or tenor recorder. The resulting sound will be fairly representative of Renaissance color.

Orchesographie (1588)

Listen to the River

Listen to the effect of the moving fifths accompanying this American folk melody,
perhaps played on alto metallophone to accompany the alto glockenspiel melody.

Trad., American

Rondo

This rondo offers the opportunity to play with a variety of color combinations and
uses three accompaniment styles explored in this book.

Jane Frazee

D.C. al Fine

Allegro #5 (from *Spielbuch für Xylophon II*)
Another Keetman treasure, this piece will sound best played by soprano xylophone
accompanied by alto xylophone because of the tempo.

Gunild Keetman

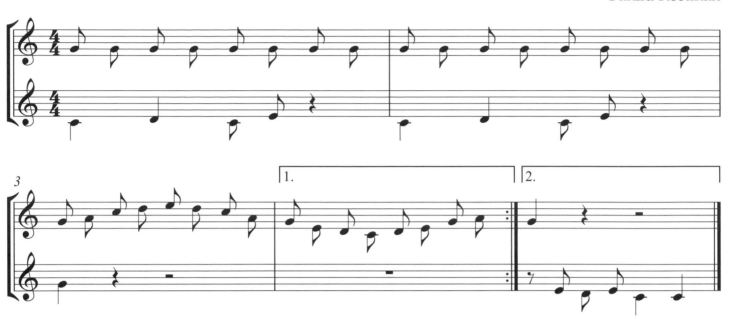

Excerpt from Allegro (from *Spielstücke für kleines Schlagwerk*)
You and your students will have fun mixing a variety of colors to perform this piece,
but xylophones will be the best choice if the tempo is fast.

Gunild Keetman

CODA

A book that addresses technique and ignores teaching process is rare in Orff-Schulwerk literature. As we all know, technique is only a prerequisite to exploring sound, improvising, and becoming aware of the nature and structure of music itself. Technical facility, however, is essential to enable students to express themselves on the instruments and to perform music that encourages aesthetic satisfaction.

In spite of the emphasis on technical development in this book, I want to end on a pedagogical note. Contributed by Michael Chandler, the following ideas will inspire you to make your way into instrumental pieces through a teaching process that encourages student success at every step.

Michael writes, "When I teach a melody, I look first for the easiest motives or phrases—especially those that repeat. We learn to play them first, and leave space for the more difficult motives or phrases. Next, I fill in the spaces by tapping my mallets to show the rhythm, and my students provide text words to illustrate it (e.g. 'walk, jog-ging, pear, ap-ple, wa-ter-mel-on'). My students then notate the rhythm of the 'mystery phrases' with rhythm cards, or they tell me how to arrange the cards. Next, they play the rhythm they have discovered on only ONE bar, alternating mallets if appropriate. As this is integrated into the context with the easier motives/phrases, I expand or limit the parameters of the bars that they may use to play this rhythm until the only possibilities remaining are those that are in the melody as written. In the meantime, they have explored and improvised MANY alternate ways to play the melodic rhythm and had LOTS of experience with mallet dexterity."

Here is how that process applies to Instrumental Piece #7, page 99 of *Music for Children I.*

Orff/Keetman

"My students can immediately play the C-G-C-G motive as it occurs in measures 1 and 3. I fill in the space by tapping 'jog-ging jog-ging walk walk' with my mallets. They determine the rhythm of both missing parts and notate them using rhythm cards. Next, they play the C-G-C-G motive as written when it occurs and choose ONE bar for the 'mystery part' (for example, second measure ALL on D or whatever bar they choose).

"Now that they can play the second measure all on one bar, where is a good place to move to another bar? The students might answer 'walk, walk.' So 'jogging jogging' could be played on E and 'walk walk' on D, another bar that is a logical choice not too far away. Where could we add even one more bar so that we're using three? How about playing the first 'walk' on one bar and the second 'walk' on a different one?

"Next, let's play some simple four note-in-a-row patterns for 'jogging jogging.' Try to find logical patterns that are easy to sing. After we've explored a number of choices, I start refining them to develop the tune as given. So now they will play a solution that can occur on *la*, *sol*, or *mi* and work until the melody is realized.

"For the teacher with limited time, this is just one way to show how a melody can be taught. I decided to be less dogmatic about alternating hands while playing after seeing Keetman's technique from the 1950s where she and her students played C-D-E with the left hand and G-A with the right hand. In most cases, the students will naturally find musical sticking patterns that work for them, and when they don't the teacher can provide assistance."

Michael's teaching process involves separating pitch from rhythm patterns to encourage student success from the beginning. Most importantly, the students discover the patterns for themselves, as they slowly uncover the intervals and rhythms of the melody. This approach delivers two important benefits: it encourages students to understand the way melodies work and it promotes skill in playing instruments.

Your students will find that they can discover melodies as illustrated in Michael's lesson if they have developed mallet skills sufficient to encourage concentration on musical, rather than technical matters. That is what you have been carefully addressing as you worked through the pieces in this book; building technical expertise that promotes artistic ensemble playing. For, as all musicians know, technique is not the end, but rather the means to promote the joy and satisfaction of making music. In a classroom setting, skill competence enables your students to fully explore the rich variety of enchanting instrumental sounds and expressive opportunities that are inspired by *Playing Together*.

Appendix
Ranges of Instruments

Ranges of Bar Instruments

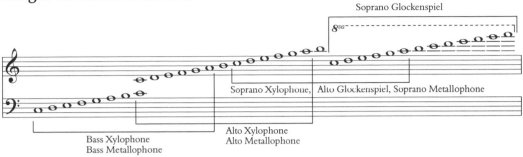

All bar instruments are notated:
(Only AX and AM sound actual notated pitch)

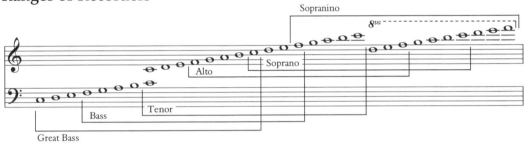

Ranges of Recorders

MELODY SOURCES

1. ENJOYING SOUNDS
Exploring Instrumental Color

Old Pond	Frazee, Jane: *Strawberry Fair*, Minneapolis: Schmitt Publications, 1977, p. 14.
Spring Rain	*Ibid.*, p. 11.

2. PLAYING ACCOMPANIMENTS
Hands Together: Octaves

German Folk Melody	Crowe, Edgar, Lawton, Annie & Gillies Whittaker, W., (comp. & ed.): *The Folk Song Sight Singing Series Book 1* Oxford: Oxford University Press, 1933, p. 2.
Ich Spring an Diesem Ring	Frazee, Jane with Kreuter, Kent: *Discovering Orff*, New York: Schott Music Corp., 1987, p. 106.
All Around the Buttercup	Boshkoff, Ruth: *All Around the Buttercup*, New York Schott Music Corp., 1984, p. 15.
Green Bough	Frazee: *Strawberry Fair*, p. 6.

Hands Together: Drones

Filles à Marier	Dolmetsch, Mabel: *Dances of England and France*, New York: Da Capo Press, 1976, p. 21.
Triory de Bretagne	Frazee, Jane: *Old Music For Young Players*, St. Paul St. Albans Press, 1985, p. 7.
Latvian Lullaby (adapted)	*Orff Instrument Handbook*, Morristown NJ: Silver Burdett, 1988, p. 19.
Moonrise	Frazee: *Strawberry Fair*, p. 22.

Hands in Alternation: Octaves

Breton Folk Melody	Crowe, Lawton & Gillies Whittaker: *Folk Song Sight Singing Series I*, p. 3.
Keetman Piece #8	Keetman, Gunild: *Erstes Spiel am Xylophon*, Mainz: B. Schott's Söhne, 1969, p. 8.
Branle	Dolmetsch: *Dances of England and France*, p. 62.
When the Sun Wakes Up	Frazee: *Strawberry Fair*, p. 16.

Hands in Alternation: Drones

Ungaresca	Kunzman, Caroline & Rempel, Ursula: *A Renaissance Banquet*, London: Schott Music Corp., 1996, p. 23.
Long Summer Day	Brocklehurst, Brian: *Pentatonic Song Book*, London: Schott Music Corp., 1968, p. 16.
Tourdion Basse Dance	Kunzman & Rempel: *A Renaissance Banquet*, p. 20.
Whistle Daughter Whistle	Early, Craig: *Something Told the Wild Geese*, New York: Schott Music Corp., 1988, p. 9.

Hands Together: Moving to Adjacent Pitches (Octaves)

Instrumental Piece	Orff, Carl & Keetman, Gunild: *Orff-Schulwerk Music for Children, Vol. II* (English ed. by Margaret Murray), London: Schott & Co. Ltd., 1959, p. 87.
Elizabethan Inspiration	Jane Frazee

Hands Together: Moving to Adjacent Pitches (Fifths)

Lullaby	Jane Frazee
Prendes I garde	Frazee: *Old Music for Young Players*, p. 1.

Moving Drone: Fifth Moves

Instrumental Piece #1	Orff & Keetman: *Music for Children II*, p. 9.
Roses	Brocklehurst: *Pentatonic Song Book*, p. 34.
No Sky At All	Frazee: *Strawberry Fair*, p. 20.

Moving Drone: Tonic Moves

Melody #11	Orff & Keetman: *Music for Children II*, p. 20.

Ring Around The Rosie	Boshkoff, Ruth: *Ring Around, Sing Around*, New York: Schott Music Corp., 1988, p. 2.

Dominant Shift: Drone Moves to Dominant Octave

Babylon's Falling	Steen, Arvida: *Exploring Orff*, New York: Schott Music Corp., 1992, p. 160.
British Folk Song	Crowe, Lawton & Gillies Whittaker: *Folk Song Sight Singing Series 1*, p. 11.
Didn't My Lord	Brocklehurst: *Pentatonic Song Book*, p. 42.

Hand Crossing: Left Crosses, Right Stable

Instrumental Piece #29	Orff, Carl & Keetman, Gunild: *Orff-Schulwerk Music for Children, Vol. I* (English ed. by Margaret Murray), 1958, p. 110.
Folk Dance	Carley, Isabel: *Recorders With Orff Ensemble*, New York: Schott Music Corp., 1984, p. 7.
Down Came a Lady	Gonzol, David: *Round the Corner and Away We Go*, New York: Schott Music Corp., 2005, p. 6.

Hand Crossing: Right Crosses, Left Stable

Cut the Cake	Boshkoff: *Ring Around, Sing Around*, p. 11.
Melody #7	Orff & Keetman: *Music for Children II*, p. 47.

3. PLAYING MELODIES

Steps

One Step at a Time	Jane Frazee
Come Be Merry	Frazee, Jane: *Orff Schulwerk Today*, Mainz: Schott Music Corp., 2006, p. 46.
La Cloche	Frazee: *Discovering Orff*, p. 133.
Sleepy Head	Jane Frazee

Skips

The Absent F	Jane Frazee
Peter Peter Pumpkin Eater	Traditional
Crooked Man	Traditional
The B Section	Elizabethan melody (adap. Jane Frazee)

Repeated Notes

The A Section	Elizabethan melody (adap. Jane Frazee)
Keetman Piece #12	Frazee, Jane: *Discovering Keetman*, New York: Schott Music Corp., 1998, p. 13.
Melody #17	Orff & Keetman: *Music for Children I*, p. 104.
Ungaresca	Regner, Hermann (Coordinator): Orff-Schulwerk *Music for Children American Edition, Vol. III*, New York: Schott Music Corp., 1980, p. 4.

Steps, Skips, and Repeated Notes

Branle de Champaigne	Frazee: *Old Music for Young Players*, p. 8.
Keetman Piece #8	Keetman, Gunild: *Spielbuch für Xylophon I*, Mainz: B. Schott's Söhne, 1965, p. 6.
Keetman Piece #22	Keetman: *Erstes Spiel am Xylophon*, p. 14.
Keetman Piece #27	Keetman: *Spielbuch für Xylophon I*, p. 12.

4. PLAYING TWO-PART INSTRUMENTAL PIECES

Canon #37	Orff & Keetman: *Music for Children I*, p. 122.
Pavan	Dolmetsch: *Dances of England and France*, p. 88.
Listen to the River	Locke, Eleanor: *Sail Away*, New York: Boosey & Hawkes, 1981, p. 122.
Rondo	Jane Frazee
Allegro #5	Keetman, Gunild: *Spielbuch für Xylophon II*, Mainz: B. Schott's Söhne, 1966, p. 8.
Allegro	Keetman, Gunild: *Spielstucke für Kleines Schlagwerk*, London: Schott & Co. Ltd., 1953, p. 25.

CODA

Instrumental Piece #7	Orff & Keetman: *Music for Children I*, p. 99.

Orff-Schulwerk American Edition

MAIN VOLUMES

Music for Children 1	Pre-School	SMC 12
Music for Children 2	Primary	SMC 6
Music for Children 3	Upper Elementary	SMC 8

SUPPLEMENTARY PUBLICATIONS

AFRICAN SONGS FOR SCHOOL AND COMMUNITY
(Robert Kwami)   SMC 551
A selection of 12 songs including traditional material and original compositions by the author.

THE ANCIENT FACE OF NIGHT (Gerald Dyck)   SMC 553
A collection of original songs and instrumental pieces for SATB chorus and Orff instruments. The cycle of songs has both astronomical and musical influences. (Chorus Part: SMC 553-01)

ANIMAL CRACKER SUITE AND OTHER POEMS
(Deborah A. Imiolo-Schriver)   SMC 561
A set of four original poems arranged for speech chorus, body percussion and percussion ensemble. Twenty-one additional original poems are included for teachers and students to make their own musical settings.

ALL AROUND THE BUTTERCUP (Ruth Boshkoff)   SMC 24
These folk song arrangements are organized progressively, each new note being introduced separately.

CHIPMUNKS, CICADAS AND OWLS (Natalie Sarrazin)   SMC 552
Twelve native American children's songs from different regions.

CIRCUS RONDO (Donald Slagel)   SMC 73
A stylized circus presentation using music, movement, speech and improvisational technique, for various Orff instruments, recorders and voices.

CROCODILE AND OTHER POEMS (Ruth Pollock Hamm)   SMC 15
A collection of verses for use as choral speech within the elementary school. Included are ideas for movement, instrumental accompaniments, and proposals for related art, drama and listening activities.

DANCING SONGS (Phillip Rhodes)   SMC 35
A song cycle for voices and Orff instruments. The contemporary harmonies create a dramatic and sophisticated experience for upper elementary/middle school grades.

DE COLORES (Virginia Ebinger)   SMC 20
Folklore from the Hispanic tradition for voices, recorders and classroom percussion.

DISCOVERING KEETMAN (Jane Frazee)   SMC 547
Rhythmic exercises and pieces for xylophone by Gunild Keetman. Selected and introduced by Jane Frazee.

DOCUM DAY (Donald Slagel)   SMC 18
An olio of songs from England, Hungary, Ireland, Jamaica, the Middle East, Newfoundland, Nova Scotia, the USA. For voices, recorders and classroom percussion.

EIGHT MINIATURES (Hermann Regner)   SMC 14
Ensemble pieces for advanced players of recorders and Orff instruments which lead directly from elementary 'Music for Children'; to chamber music for recorders.

ELEMENTAL RECORDER PLAYING
(Gunild Keetman and Minna Ronnefeld) Translation by Mary Shamrock
Teacher's Book   SMC 558
This book is based on the fundamental principles of Orff-Schulwerk. The book can be used as a foundation text in an elementary music program that includes use of the recorder. It can also be employed in teaching situations that concentrate primarily upon recorder but in which ensemble playing, improvisation and singing also play an essential role.
Student's Book   SMC 559
Includes a variety of exercises, songs, pieces, improvisation exercises, canons, duets, rondos and texts to use for making rhythms and melodies.
Student's Workbook   SMC 560
Contains exercises and games for doing at home and during the music lesson. Integrated with work in the Student's Book.

FENCE POSTS AND OTHER POEMS (Ruth Pollock Hamm)   SMC 31
Texts for melodies, 'Sound Envelopes', movement and composition written by children, selected poets and the editor. Material for creative melody making and improvisation (including jazz).

FOUR PSALM SETTINGS (Sue Ellen Page)   SMC 30
For treble voices (unison and two-part) and Orff instruments.

HAVE YOU ANY WOOL? THREE BAGS FULL! (Richard Gill) SMC 29
17 traditional rhymes for voices and Orff instruments. Speech exercises, elaborate settings for Orff instruments using nursery rhymes to show how to play with texts.

HELLO CHILDREN (Shirley Salmon)   SMC 572
A collection of songs and related activities for children aged 4–9

KUKURÍKU (Miriam Samuelson)   SMC 57
Traditional Hebrew songs and dances (including Hava Nagila) arranged for voices, recorders and Orff instruments. Instructions (with diagrams) are given for the dances.

THE MAGIC FOREST (Lynn Johnson)   SMC 16
Sequenced, early childhood, music-lesson plans based on the Orff-Schulwerk approach.

PIECES AND PROCESSES (Steven Calantropio)   SMC 569
This collection of original songs, exercises, instrumental pieces, and arrangements provides fresh examples of elemental music. Along with each piece is a detailed teaching procedure designed to give music educators a collection of instructional techniques.

THE QUANGLE WANGLE'S HAT (Sara Newberry)   SMC 32
Edward Lear's delightful poem set for speaker(s), recorders and Orff instruments (with movement and dance improvisation).

¡QUIEN CANTA SU MAL ESPANTA!
Songs, Games and Dances from Latin America
(Sofia Lopez-Ibor and Verena Maschat)   SMC 568
This book presents a rich and varied selection of material from an immense geographical area, combining local traditions with foreign influences to engage and inspire teachers and students. The DVD includes demonstrations of the dances for presentation in the classroom.

THE RACCOON PHILOSOPHER
(Danai Gagne-Apostolidou and Judith Thomas-Solomon)   SMC 566
A drama in mixed meters for upper elementary grades with preparatory activities for singing, moving, playing recorder, Orff instruments and creating. The Raccoon Philosopher was inspired by thoughts on virtue by Martin Buber. As we learn from the raccoon, so we learn from the children: to be merry for no particular reason, to never for a moment be idle, and to express our needs vigorously.

RECORDERS WITH ORFF ENSEMBLE (Isabel McNeill Carley) SMC 25-27
Three books designed to fill a need for a repertoire (pentatonic and diatonic) for beginning and intermediate recorder players. Most of the pieces are intended to be both played and danced and simple accompaniments are provided.

RINGAROUND, SINGAROUND (Ruth Boshkoff)   SMC 33
Games, rhymes and folksongs for the early elementary grades, arranged in sequential order according to concepts.

ROUND THE CORNER AND AWAY WE GO (David J. Gonzol)   SMC 567
This folk song collection provides models of arrangements to be taught using Orff-Schulwerk processes. The accompanying teaching suggestions give examples of how to break down instrumental parts and sequence the presentation of them developmentally.

RRRRRO
(Polyxene Mathéy and Angelika Panagopoulos-Slavik)   SMC 79
Poetry, music and dance from Greece with Greek texts adapted for rhythmic reciting by groups accompanied by percussion and other instruments.

A SEASONAL KALEIDOSCOPE
(Joyce Coffey, Danai Gagne, Laura Koulish)   SMC 55
Original songs, poetry and stories with Orff instruments for children. Bound by a theme of seasonal changes and intended for classroom and music teachers.

SIMPLY SUNG (Mary Goetze)   SMC 23
Folk songs arranged in three parts for young singers. They include American folk songs, spirituals and Hebrew melodies.

SKETCHES IN STYLE (Carol Richards and Neil Aubrey)   SMC 19
Arrangements for classroom music. For voices, recorders and classroom percussion.

SOMETHING TOLD THE WILD GEESE (Craig Earley)   SMC 21
A collection of folksongs for unison treble voices, barred and small percussion instruments, and recorders (soprano and alto).

STREET GAMES (Gloria Fuoco-Lawson)   SMC 17
Instrumental arrangements of rhythmical hand jives based on traditional American street games.

TALES TO TELL, TALES TO PLAY
(Carol Erion and Linda Monssen)   SMC 28
Four folk tales (Indian, African, German and American Indian) retold and arranged for music and movement, with accompaniment for recorders and Orff instruments.

TEN FOLK CAROLS FOR CHRISTMAS FROM THE UNITED STATES
(Jane Frazee)   SMC 22
Settings of Appalachian and unfamiliar carols, arranged for voices, recorders and Orff instruments.

TUNES FOR YOUNG TROUBADOURS (Dianne Ladendecker)   SMC 34
Ten songs for children's voices, recorders and Orff ensemble.

WIND SONGS (Phillip Rhodes)   SMC 197
Four songs for unison voices, barred and small percussion instruments.